THE
WHITE MOUNTAINS

A Postcard Book

FALCON®

GUILFORD, CONNECTICUT
HELENA, MONTANA

AN IMPRINT OF THE GLOBE PEQUOT PRESS

A rustic fence opens up to a meadow nestled beneath the pro-
file of New Hampshire's Mount Chocorua. With an elevation
of just under 3,500 feet, Mount Chocorua is one of the most
climbed and picturesque mountains in the mountain range.

Please Place

First-Class

Stamp Here

THE WHITE MOUNTAINS

At an elevation of 6,288 feet above mean sea level, snow-covered Mount Washington in New Hampshire is the highest peak in the northeastern United States.

THE WHITE MOUNTAINS

Mountain streams, forests, high peaks, and waterfalls stretch across nearly 800,000 acres of New Hampshire and Maine in White Mountain National Forest.

THE WHITE MOUNTAINS

For the last 15,000 years, the Pemigewasset River in New Hampshire's Franconia Notch State Park has cascaded down onto solid granite, forming this natural pool known as the Basin.

Please Place

First-Class

Stamp Here

THE WHITE MOUNTAINS

From atop the Lion Head Trail in White Mountain National Park, hikers can see the Boott Spur Trail across Tuckerman Ravine in New Hampshire.

Photograph © Jerry and Marcy Monkman/www.ecophotography.com

Please Place

First-Class

Stamp Here

THE WHITE MOUNTAINS

Whitehorse Ledge near North Conway, New Hampshire, can be seen from the top of Cathedral Ledge, a spot popular with rock climbers but also accessible by road.

Please Place

First-Class

Stamp Here

THE WHITE MOUNTAINS

New Hampshire's Ellis River, which runs through Pinkham Notch in White Mountain National Forest, is known for its waterfalls.

Please Place

First-Class

Stamp Here

THE WHITE MOUNTAINS

*The beautiful Saco River Valley in New Hampshire sits among
the mountains adjacent to White Mountain National Forest.*

how spectacular it all is. Because the truth is, we are collectors of treasures, each and every one of us: We go out there, we open our hearts

THE WHITE MOUNTAINS

to savor the miracles and expand the bliss. Now send this little beauty out there so that others can get themselves a piece of the joy!

and we long for little pieces of wonder to spread around and bring back home. This is how we make our lives bigger and more fantastic; and in this crazy world of ours, we need to do everything we can

Just north of the Kancamagus Highway in New Hampshire, the Albany Bridge spans the Swift River in White Mountain National Forest.

THE WHITE MOUNTAINS

Leafy branches form a canopy over New Hampshire's West River as it flows through White Mountain National Forest into Waterville Valley.

Please Place

First-Class

Stamp Here

THE WHITE MOUNTAINS

The White Mountains are home to both sweeping valleys and wind-whipped summits.

Please Place

First-Class

Stamp Here

THE WHITE MOUNTAINS

and we long for little pieces of wonder to spread around and bring back home. This is how we make our lives bigger and more fantastic; and in this crazy world of ours, we need to do everything we can to savor the miracles and expand the bliss. Now send this little beauty out there so that others can get themselves a piece of the joy!

The lakes region of the White Mountains offers hundreds of opportunities for boating and fishing.

THE WHITE MOUNTAINS

Fields of lupine grow at the base of the mountains on a summer afternoon. The Great Gulf Wilderness is one of the finest backpacking and hiking areas of White Mountain National Forest in New Hampshire.

THE WHITE MOUNTAINS

Atop New Hampshire's Mount Washington sits a nonprofit scientific and educational observatory. It is used to study the unique meteorology and natural subarctic environment of the Mount Washington region.

THE WHITE MOUNTAINS

how spectacular it all is. Because the truth is, we are collectors of treasures, each and every one of us: We go out there, we open our hearts

and we forage for little pieces of wonder to spread around and bring back home. This is how we make our lives bigger and more fantastic; and in this crazy world of ours, we need to do everything we can

to savor the miracles and expand the bliss. Now send this little beauty out there so that others can get themselves a piece of the joy!

Franconia Brook runs through New Hampshire's Franconia Range in White Mountain National Forest.

THE WHITE MOUNTAINS

★ In the spirit of a solitary photographer taking a photo of something rare and fabulous, we—the dedicated folk of The Globe Pequot Press—offer you this nifty, galaxy-class postcard to help you remember how spectacular it all is. Because the truth is, we are collections of treasures, each and every one of us: We go out there, we open our hearts,

Mount Chocorua is visible across Chocorua Lake in New Hampshire's beautiful lakes region.

Please Place

First-Class

Stamp Here

THE WHITE MOUNTAINS

and we scrounge for little pieces of wonder to spread around and bring back home. This is how we make our lives bigger and more fantastic; and in this crazy world of ours, we need to do everything we can to savor the miracles and expand the bliss. Now send this little beauty out there so that others can get themselves a piece of the joy!

Bemis Brook cascades through Crawford Notch State Park in New Hampshire. With more than 5,700 acres, Crawford Notch abounds with waterfalls, hiking trails, and beautiful scenery.

Please Place

First-Class

Stamp Here

THE WHITE MOUNTAINS

Fall foliage is particularly brilliant along the mountain streams.

Photograph © 2004 by Tony Sweet

Please Place

First-Class

Stamp Here

THE WHITE MOUNTAINS

New Hampshire's Crawford Notch is the main passage through the center of the mountains.

Please Place

First-Class

Stamp Here

THE WHITE MOUNTAINS